the little book of

Happiness

A special little something for you

To

From

Just wanted to say…

The Little Book of Happiness

Copyright © 2015 David & Heidi Cuschieri
Images copyright © 2015 Shutterstock

All rights reserved. Other than for personal use, no part of this book may be reproduced in any way, in whole or part without the written consent of the copyright holder or publisher. This book is intended for spiritual and emotional guidance only. It is not intended to replace medical assistance or treatment.

Published by Blue Angel Publishing
80 Glen Tower Drive, Glen Waverley,
Victoria, Australia 3150
E-mail: info@blueangelonline.com
Website: www.blueangelonline.com

Blue Angel is a registered trademark of Blue Angel Gallery Pty. Ltd.

ISBN: 978-1-922161-56-7

This book originally published in Australia by The Next Big Think
www.the-next-big-think.com

DISCLAIMER
We have made every effort to ensure the quotations contained in this book have been quoted and referenced correctly. If you believe an error has been made with regards to any of the quotations in this book, please email: info@the-next-big-think.com

the little book of
Happiness

GREETING BOOK SERIES

The Secret To Purrfect Happiness

Have you ever wondered why cats purr?

It's because they have long discovered the secret to happiness. Their lives are filled with moments of relaxation, stretching, meowing, sleeping, purring and more sleeping. They don't worry about the share price of cat food on the stock market or think back to their unhappy kittenhood.

In your own hectic life, it is important that you take time to understand what true happiness is.

Many of us spend our lives chasing our own tails searching for happiness, thinking that it is something outside of ourselves. Whether it be accumulating money, power, wealth and possessions, expecting others to give it to us, searching the past or looking to the future for it.

But true happiness may be closer to you than you think.

Whether you are rich or poor, black or white, short or tall, it doesn't matter at all. Happiness doesn't discriminate. What some of the happiest people in the world have discovered are the secrets that cats have known since time began.

Let us share with you one of these secrets.

What many of us don't understand is that happiness is already inside of us. All we need to do is recognize this and make the choice to be happy or not. We can make this decision in a heart beat. You see, true happiness is about living in the present, about being in the moment.

Spend time with cats; study them. Listen closely to their purring. You may just be listening to the gentle sound of pure happiness.

You need not look any further for true happiness; it has always been inside of you. You need not wait for happiness any longer. Happiness is always and will always be, here and now.

Sometimes just one inspirational or touching word can be all it takes for us to shift our mindset from sadness and anxiety to happiness. We hope that through the uplifting words and beautiful images in this book, you can come to your own realization about what happiness really is.

To your happiness!
David and Heidi

Happiness

is always taking the time to smell the

roses.

Heidi McLachlan

> Happiness comes from the word *'happen'*.
> Happen derives from the word *'hap'*.
> Hap means *chance* or *luck*.
> We are taught to believe that happiness is hap-hazard. How hazardous indeed our existence is if we fail to take responsibility for the happiness in our lives and leave it to chance.
>
> *David Cuschieri*

begin it.

Boldness has genius,
        power and
              magic in it.

Johann Wolfgang von Goethe

Life doesn't require that we be the

best

...only that we try our best.

H. Jackson Brown Jr.

I wish people could achieve

what they think would bring them happiness

in order for them to realize that

that's not really what happiness is.

Alanis Morissette

It's not how much we **have,** but how much we **enjoy** that makes happiness.

Charles H. Spurgeon

Happiness is contagious...
when you reflect happiness,
then all others around you catch
the happy bug and are happy too.

Jennifer Leese

Everyone who got where he **is** had to begin where he **was**.

Charles H. Spurgeon

Trust thyself;

every heart vibrates to that iron string.

Ralph Waldo Emerson

Worry

doesn't help tomorrow's troubles,

but it does ruin

today's happiness.

Unknown

You will never be happier than you expect.

To change your happiness, change your expectation.

Bette Davis

Those who bring sunshine in the lives of others, cannot keep it from themselves.

James M. Barrie

Happiness often sneaks in through a door you didn't know you left open.

John Barrymore

We're born to be happy, all of us.

Alfred Sutro

If only we'd stop trying to be happy
we'd have a pretty good time.

Edith Wharton

 Happy thoughts are not as hard as you might think. All it takes is a matter of changing your attitude and mindset and this is easier than you think.

Heidi McLachlan

There are some days when I think I'm going to die from an overdose of satisfaction.

Salvador Dali

[Nobody really cares if you're miserable, so you might as well be happy.

Cynthia Nelms

No one has ever injured his

eyesight

by looking on the bright side

of things.

Unknown

{ The true secret of happiness lies in taking a genuine interest in all the details of daily life and elevating them to an art.

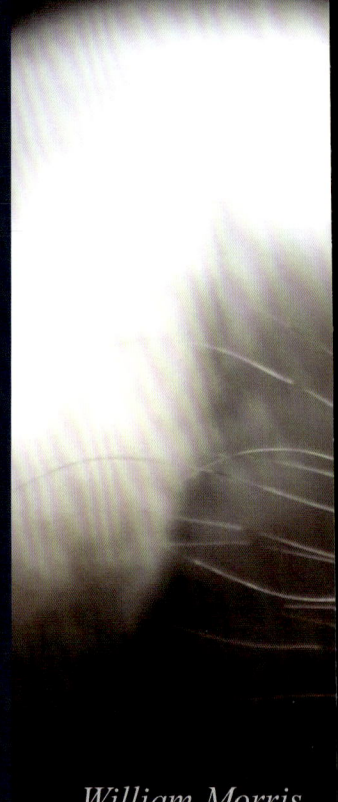

William Morris

She thinks happiness is a mat that sits on her doorway.

Rob Thomas, "3am"

Real elation is when you feel you could touch a star without standing on tiptoe.

Doug Larson

Happiness doesn't just happen.
It needs to be sustained by a careful diet
of good thoughts, great company and giving.
Happiness is about exercising your
biggest muscle daily – your mind.

Happiness is a

perfume

you cannot pour on others

without getting a few drops

on yourself.

Ralph Waldo Emerson

It is only possible to live happily ever

after on a day-to-day basis.

Margaret Bonnano

[The best way to cheer yourself up
is to try to cheer somebody else up.]

Mark Twain

Much happiness

is overlooked because

it doesn't cost anything.

Unknown

In every life we have some trouble.
When you worry, you make it double.
Don't worry, be happy...

Bobby McFerrin, "Don't Worry Be Happy"

Don't worry,

be happy ....

The pursuit of happiness is a most ridiculous phrase.

If you pursue happiness you'll never find it.

C.P. Snow

Happiness...is not a destination:

it is a manner of traveling.

Happiness is not an end in itself:

It is a by-product of working,

playing,

loving

and living.

Haim Ginott

When one door of happiness closes, another opens; but often we look so long at the closed door that we do not see the one which has been opened for us.

Helen Keller

Happiness is mostly a by-product of doing what makes us feel fulfilled.

Dr. Benjamin Spock

Happiness comes only from
appreciating what you have right now.
You can even be happy by
appreciating your troubles
because they are helping to
build your character.

Harriet Meyerson

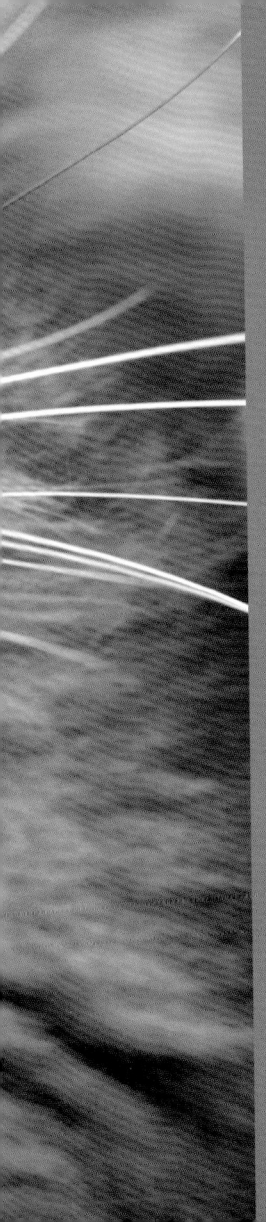

Those who can laugh

    without cause

        have either found

the true meaning of happiness

    or have gone

        stark raving mad.

Norm Papernick

[Happiness is never stopping to think if you are.]

Palmer Sondreal

We are as **happy** as

we make up our

minds

to be.

Abraham Lincoln

You will never be happy if you

continue to search

for what happiness consists of.

You will never live

if you are looking for

the meaning of life.

Albert Camus

Happiness is moment to moment.

It is always now.

David Cuschieri

If you want to be happy, be.

Leo Tolstoy

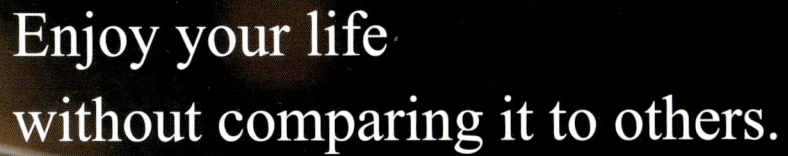

Enjoy your life
without comparing it to others.

Marquis de Condorcet

About the Authors

David and Heidi Cuschieri are the best-selling authors of many inspirational books on happiness, mindfulness and well-being. They believe we each carry within us our own wisdom gained from life's experiences. The couple's vision is to connect people in meaningful ways through their words and inspiration.

Their website **The School of Happiness** aims to help others find their own path to inner happiness providing guideposts along the way.

They live on the subtropical Gold Coast of Australia.

Find out more by visiting **www.davidandheidicuschieri.com**

Thank You

We have brought together the words and the images of others, to send out special messages to touch the hearts and lives of people the world over.

Thank you to all who have made this book possible – the people whose words of wisdom fill the pages; the photographers whose images give us joy and wonder; the printers for their attention to detail and assistance; the distributors for their guidance, passion and belief; the retailers for their support; and last but not least, to the gift givers and receivers who will pay it forward and carry on the essence of what The Little Books are all about.

We say thank you and are grateful to you all.

More inspiring titles by the authors:

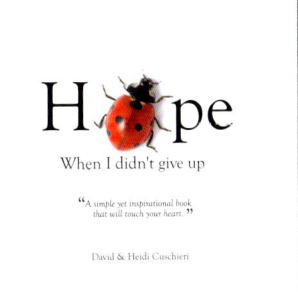

This book is in your hands for a reason

We don't see our books as mere commodities to be traded, but receptacles of energy. This chain of energy began long before any of us were born and we are grateful for these people whose lives, experiences and lessons have been expressed by the words that fill the pages of this book.

A book is more than a collection of printed words and images on pieces of paper bound together. A book holds incredible energy. Thoughts are powerful and when put into words they can transform people's lives and even the course of humanity.

The family of people around us who help make these little books possible, also enrich and transform the lives of others. From the photographers who take the pictures, to the local bookstore owner who places the books on his shelves.

We encourage the giver to present this book to someone special holding it with two hands and arms outstretched. To gently hand a gift to someone in this way is an Asian custom of respect. This connection brings people together in times when it may be needed most and continues the cycle of energy.

May this book find its way into your hands and heart.